OBLIVION

TIRTHA. C

To,

Dear Tindu.

I hope you find your true self soon and I pray happiness finds you soon.

Contents

Contents

Contents

Contents

Foreword

Oblivion means the state of being unaware. *As a human, there will be moments when you wish for everything to either get over soon or to stop at a particular moment. Either way it will be your loss.*

If you want time to pass on quickly, you will not be able to enjoy the present moments. If you want time to stop by, you will be stuck forever.

To move on and to change with the changing times, is the key to a successful survival. However, on this journey, I hope you won't lose yourself. Rather I hope you acknowlegde your inner self and find out the true you.

What if everything you ever wished for,

Simply wanted to avoid you.

What if all the success and fortune you wanted,

Was not meant for you?

What if all the hardships and suffering was meant for you?

So that you would be an inspiration for the others.

What if?

They say that the world is kind,

They say that the world knows to care,

They say that the world know how to share,

They say that the world knows the language of love.

What a lie!

At times we need something more than a mirror,

To see who we really are.

But it doesn't help.

What helps is to look in the eyes of the person,

Who loves you.

Those eyes will show you,

Your true self.

Secrets aren't made to be kept hidden,

Same as promises aren't made to be kept.

People say time heals,

The truth being it doesn't.

It teaches you,

To ignore and move on.

The tales tell us about the story of the hero and the villain,

Little do we realize that

the actual one at fault was the author,

That made them cross their paths?

Emotions are given,

To be expressed.

But to survive in this world,

One needs to be emotionless.

If the heart were that easy to understand,

Wouldn't everyone be a cardiologist?

If people knew how to love,

So many hearts wouldn't be broken every day.

Every hardship makes you strong,

Every wound leaves behind a scar.

That's why everyone is left heartbroken,

Until they learn to heal their own scars.

At the end of the day,

You only have yourself and no one else.

It's always the coldest time of your life.

That people you look up the most to,

Leave you.

Always.

Animals are the best creatures that display affection.

They cling to you if they like you

And detest you if they don't.

The point to be noted, humans are classified as animals.

If people understood what we want and don't,

By just looking into eyes.

Then there would be no use of sign languages.

Authors do their best,

In trying to give the readers a perfect story.

A story that can't be true.

If sorry had made any difference,

Wouldn't all crimes and mistakes be forgiven?

Every lock has a key,

To keep secrets.

Wish the mouth and thoughts had locks,

So that all the secrets would be safely guarded.

First they give stress,

Then ask the reason.

You!

You are the reason sire!

Dressing all the time,

And instructed to smile.

Trying to impress,

The society simply just sucks.

If being broken into pieces was like,

Taking sips of slow poison.

I think that I might be,

Immune to this poison.

Failing in love,

And excelling at everything else.

What sins did I commit?

How to break these spells?

People don't give up their lives,

After losing to other people.

People give up,

After losing to their inner self.

Love can give two results:

1. Happiness

That makes you forget every pain in your life.

2. Pain

That makes you forget every happiness in your life.

If you have to beg someone for their,

Time, attention, love.

You don't matter to them any longer.

If you want to hurt me,

Hurt me little by little.

So when you leave me,

I won't feel anything.

The wind blows lightly,

Tapping gently on the face.

Where once my mom caressed me,

So that I didn't make a mistake.

Be nice.

Be cool.

Be kind.

Be lovable.

To yourself.

Prioritize yourself first.

Your brown eyes,

That sparkles in the sun.

Your cheerful smile,

After some fun.

You don't know how dangerous your charms can be,

For someone such as me.

And yet again,

I would search for you.

For your existence,

Is a blessing in disguise.

If they truly love you,

No matter the obstacles,

The pain, disappoints and struggles,

They will be with you till the end.

If you tend to give more,

Lend more, care more,

Protect more, love more.

Be ready to get hurt more.

In the era of emails,

Tweets, snaps, instagram DMs.

I just want to write you letters.

In the future,

If your kid asks them to tell you a horror story.

Tell them your life story,

That would be enough to scare the shit outta them.

If you don't intend to love someone,

Unconditionally.

You have no right to stay

In their lives.

Flowers wilt,

And bloom again.

Trees shed their leaves,

And grow them again.

When the heart breaks,

It will heal again.

There is nothing in the world,

That cannot be mended after being broken.

The worse wounds and the deepest scars,

All will heal.

If fairy tales were true,

I fear I am the side character.

That wishes to be the main character.

Without knowing the entire story was about the side character.

Why is the money tree called a money tree,

When it doesn't grow money,

Or attracts it as a magnet?

Men deserve flowers too,

Men deserve lockets too,

Men deserve to be taken to shopping too,

Men deserve proposals too.

Men have the right to every happiness that women want to experience too.

What's the use of trapping light in a bulb,

When you have already lost your inner spark?

The bulb can illuminate an area,

But the light that was to be spread by you,

Has already vanished.

I don't get people that despise handmade gifts.

Throughout the entire process, right from the point they started making it,

Till the last part.

Their only thought was you.

YOU.

Every story has a hero,

That was misunderstood,

And was cruelly named as the

'Villain'.

Why do grades matter?

Why does status matter?

Why do looks matter?

When all that matters is the end result.

The only answers are either,

Yes or No.

There is nothing in between.

There is nothing such as Maybe.

Be with people,

Who treat you as a choice.

Not an option.

The only ways to stop pain,

Is either,

Search and embrace happiness.

Or

Stop feeling anything at all.

Teens acting as adults,

And adults acting as teens,

Reminds of the wolf,

Beneath the skin of a sheep.

At then at times,

Even the soulmates,

Are not meant to be together.

People aren't scared to fall in love,

People are scared about what comes after it.

Will it be endless happiness?

Or will it be tormented suffering?

At times,

We wish for the happiness of those,

In whose life,

We don't exist anymore.

One sided love is pure,

Long distance relationship is purer.

But dating to marry,

That's the purest.

It is okay,

Not to say everything.

Remember,

Not everything needs to be answered.

It's always the sad endings that people remember.

No one remembers the happy ever after ends.

That's cause people always prefer tragedy,

Over the fantasy.

Because it's more realistic.

We mature before time,

We just don't realize it.

Just as we love before time,

And don't realize it.

It's never easy to excel every time.

It's never easy to stand after you fall.

But when it comes to proving your worth,

You should exceed your own expectations.

Birds fly high,

Not because they have wings.

But because they were pushed from a height,

And had to flap their wings,

Just to survive.

And at the end of the day,

I'd still want to update you about myself.

And you'd read those messages,

Thinking, 'this mess belongs to me.'

In a time where people give you,

Bouquet of flowers,

I want someone,

To grow those flowers with me,

Until we are buried under them.

I had fallen in love,

Many times before I met you.

It would be wrong to say,

That I wouldn't be able to love anyone after you.

But I wouldn't be able to love anyone,

The way I loved you.

If doing things for your love,

Is like taking bits of your pieces to complete the other person,

It isn't love anymore.

It's sacrifice.

When

Expectations hurt,

People hurt,

Words hurt,

Love hurts.

That is when,

Pain heals.

The relationships based on lies,

Don't last.

When was the last time,

You didn't lie in a relation?

Ghosting people is fun,

Until the one person,

You want the most at a particular moment,

Ghosts you.

People be detesting snakes,

And then,

Being one their own selves.

Counting stars isn't a waste of time.

What's waste of a time,

Is hoping that the person you are willing to count the stars for,

Will actually believe you.

Some people are good with relationship advices,

Like they have experienced it countless times.

When the truth is,

Their books and one sided love's have taught them a lot more,

Than the practical relations would have.

And then there are girls,

Who hold a book in one hand,

And a sword in another.

Who sings the songs of love,

But carry hearts of stone.

Who smile with kindness to others,

And threaten others with the same smile.

To love is okay,

To be heartbroken is okay.

To be in pain is okay.

But what's not okay,

Is to beg for love to someone who doesn't deserve you.

Dignity is all that matters.

People can understand the meaning,

Between two digits.

But still can't figure out,

How to read between the lines.

Calling each other by your nicknames,

Is fun and sweet.

But nothing can beat the feeling,

Of being called by your name.

Your name, being called by the one,

You cherish the most.

Maybe the villains of the story,

Are actually people who wanted to be loved.

But because the people loved the hero more,

All they wanted to do was replace the hero

And gain the love.

Not realizing, that replacing someone,

Is just being a substitute for him.

Not being your true self,

But a mere shadow of him.

Enough of deaths like Romeo and Juliet,

Who died due to love,

Need new stories,

Who kill for love.

In this world,

Your struggles, pain, hardwork,

Nothing matter.

All that matters,

Is the result.

But then, hasn't the world always being a cruel place.

Authors make us fall in love and sympathize,

With the characters so easily.

And then eliminate them from the story,

As they were nothing but mere puppets.

Hasn't love,

Always being an illusion?

At the end of the day,

No one deserves the best version of you.

No one except,

Yourself.

If you start getting used to their company,

Always take out some time alone for yourself.

Cause if they leave you,

You should be able to say, "Fine I will watch movie alone."

If they love that sweet side of yours,

Make sure to display the worst side of yours in the most horrible way.

That way you'll know,

If they like you,

Or they love you.

Maybe it was all written in the stars,

Maybe it was all visible,

Maybe it was all meant to be,

But you were blind.

Maybe songwriters are fortune tellers.

Cause if not,

How could they write songs,

That describe our lives so right?

And at times,

The real happiness was hidden in the journey

And not in the destination.

Start of every healthy relation,

Starts at home.

When parents, siblings and people,

Love and support children,

They learn to spread love all over.

Two of the worst feelings,

Guilt and regret.

Guilt of not doing something,

And the regret of not doing it.

They say,

Falling in love makes one lose their sanity.

Them being the same people,

Who drink to lose consciousness.

Capturing moments on camera,

Is more important to some.

Rather than living it.

We really do not understand,

The worth of some people,

Until they leave you,

For the other.

If there was a choice between,

Success and love.

Choose success.

For we don't know if success comes to people in love, but

Love comes to successful people.

Meeting new people is always so fun,

You get to discover,

That there are people who are dumber than you.

And if you are unlucky, then you find the smatter ones.

We never want people to disappear from our lives.

All we want is to erase their memories

From our lives.

Maybe God is the author of our story,

But that doesn't mean that we forget,

That we are the main character.

And so, eventually,

Things will work out for us in the end.

If time would be stopped,

Then may it be stopped,

When I am at my lowest.

For when I stand again,

I remember the pain that I experienced that long.

People who like eating spicy,

Have their reason of eating it,

As their life,

Has no spice in it.

The most satisfying 3 words,

Is not,

I Love You.

It's,

I, Me, Myself.

If I stop smiling to you,

It doesn't mean I am pissed at you.

I am just tired of,

Wearing this fake mask where ever I go.

If my appointment with God

Is fixed earlier than yours,

And I leave for it without you.

I'd hope you bring me flowers,

Whenever it rains.

So that along with you,

The heavens would cry for me too.